Catching
Light

Catching Light

poems

Kathryn Stripling Byer

Louisiana State University Press ✤ Baton Rouge 2002

First printing

11 10 09 08 07 06 05 04 03 02

5 4 3 2 1

Designer: Amanda McDonald Scallan
Typeface: Sabon
Printer and binder: Thomson-Shore, Inc.

Library of Congress Cataloging-in-Publication Data

Byer, Kathryn Stripling.
    Catching light : poems / Kathryn Stripling Byer.
        p. cm.
    ISBN 08071-2769-8 (cloth : alk. paper) — ISBN 0-8071-2770-1 (pbk. : alk. paper)
    I. Title.

PS3569.T6965 C38 2002
811'.54—dc21

                                                                2001038989

The author gratefully acknowledges the editors of the following publications, in which some of the poems herein first appeared, sometimes in different forms: A! Magazine: "Music Lesson"; Arts and Letters: "Hoot Owl," "Looking Out," number 5 from "In the Photograph Gallery"; Asheville Poetry Review: "Nemesis"; Brightleaf: "Eve Sings to the Okra" (as "Gumbo"); Calyx: "Old"; Crab Orchard Review: "Her Porch," "Unanswerable"; Shenandoah: "Nocturne," "Trunk"; Solo: "Eve"; Southern Review: "Wisteria"; Sow's Ear: "Cold Spell," "Letting" (as "Pas de Deux"), "Vanity"; Tar River Poetry: "Wedding" (as "Old Maid"), "Open Casket," "Pearls," "Tired."

Seven of the poems herein were first printed in Eve, a chapbook from Bluenose Press, Chapel Hill, N.C., 1998. Eighteen of these poems, along with photographs, were finalists for the 1997 Taylor-Lange Prize from the Center for Documentary Studies, Durham, N.C. They were privately printed in a limited edition titled Evelyn.

My thanks to Penelope Scambly Schott for her assistance in revising this manuscript. I also thank Lenoir-Rhyne College, Hickory, North Carolina, where I spent the spring of 1999 as Writer-in-Residence. Many of the poems in this book were begun while there. My special thanks to Rand Brandes for the invitation and hospitality. My gratitude to the Hambidge Center for Creative Arts in Rabun Gap, Ga., for giving me the time to work on this collection.

For my mother, Bernice Campbell Stripling,
and my mother-in-law, Ina Mae Byer

To the memory of Marie Beaudry Lucas
and Betty Bell, our "Evelyn"

Love fiercely, you say.
Stand back from the door.
—*Cecilia Woloch, from* "Light & Aching"

CONTENTS

{1}

Time collected dust
Settled into corners
Filled me with a hunger
nothing could contain . . .
Soon days began
to catch light.
—Marie Beaudry Lucas,
from "Instead Of"

IN THE PHOTOGRAPH GALLERY

1.
"She looks like a ghost,"
somebody says,
staring at me
walking my yard of an evening,
if yard you could call it now,
honeysuckle vines running wild
and the blackberries leaping from one side
of dark to another.

I walk among photographs
wondering who it is these people think
I am.

"Who is she?"
a child hanging on to her mother's skirt
asks, as if she is frightened
by what she sees. "Just a little old lady,"
her mother soothes.

"That's all she is."

2.
Am I breathing?
Lying here on the grass
with my face
to the ground?

Does my hand move?
An ant crawl across it?
A bird's feather fall?

Shake me.
Nudge my arm.
Tell me to wake up
and say something.

3.
On my hands and knees,
digging awhile in what used to be
garden, my back caught a moment in light
like each one of these ferns lifting
out of the leafmold,

I can't see that blazing
white sea-swell beyond me
keep coming

while here in the undertow
I grip my trowel,
the afternoon fading,
the pool of my life
growing still.

4.
Even up here in the attic
enough light comes through
to make holding this hoop skirt of white
net I wore to the dance
one more luminous moment.

If I tried to dance
in it now, it would tear from its ribbing,
collapse,
perhaps I would trip over it,
tumble into
the rubble of too long a life.

The daylight as seen through
its netting looks
dreamlike as first love,
the lights on the dance floor
beginning to lower,
the slow-dance we waited
all night for
about to begin.

5.
How many women
have sat as I see myself
sit in this car going
nowhere, their eyes looking out
at the same small-town streets
or the same fields
a father or husband has tilled
while they inhale
the odor of vinyl
and motor oil,
turning the radio dial
through a rainbow
of static till they hear
a woman's voice
wailing all the way down
from Chicago
the same old
sad sing-along,
Somebody done
gone and left me here,
night coming on.

6.
A place for everything . . .
but how can everything stay always
in one place?

 Are there that many places?

And where is my place?
In this mirror
I don't want to look into?

There always around me
the dead flowers
curlicue over
the walls as if to say *Here
is your only
true place.*

*The reflection
you see in your own eyes.*

7.

What a clutter my days
have come down to: that lampshade
aslant on its axis,
the desk running over
with letters and bills,
all the pages I've ripped out of one magazine
or another. I sit
inside rooms spilling
over with things   '
while the sun moves across the floor,
turning to light
all that lies in its path, as I am
hair by hair
kindling, the whole of me
waiting to go up in one burst of late
afternoon torching everything.

8.
White feather
fallen or blown here
as if from some raggedy cloud
passing almost as fast as these
days I grab hold of,

what wing did you
stray from?
What message
or warning

do you bring
me, standing here clutching
you, white hand-
me-down
feather
I hold like a quill pen
to write upon nothingness?

9.
This window keeps watching
me walking away through the weeds.

In my old bedroom shoes
I go shuffling.

Come back,
I breathe onto the glass.

Write my name
on the curtain my breath makes a little while.

Eve. . . . Evelyn. Where are you going
without me?

10.
You think in the dark
I am nobody.

Open the door.
Do you see who I am?

Tell me,
you who see only the back of me,

how does my face look
confronting the light?

{2}

But how did it happen
that I was the little Resi
and suddenly I am the old woman!
Die alte Frau, die alte Marschallin!
—from *Der Rosenkavalier*

OLD

I never liked curtains.
I wanted my windows left free
so that I could see through

to the other side: limbs white
as ghost-lassos
all tangled up in themselves

and the wind always teasing
the patterns around.

Now I worry the difference
between what I see
in this mirror and out
there. But what does it matter?

I look into both.
See the same woman's life all around me.

Old.
Old as creation.

LETTING

go, the leaves try
to teach
me a thing or
two yet
about dying,
as if I have not
seen enough
of that falling
away to last
lifetimes of
wondering what if
I crumpled
and fell
to the ground,
who would look
at me, murmuring
oh, what a
graceful
departure, that
old woman floating
so gently
down onto
the compost pile.

FALLOW

Lying down where the garden once grew,
I imagine my flesh turning
back into dirt
while I ask myself what can
an old woman grow
from her bones
and her blood that could
root its way deep
enough into those memories
nobody knows how
to see till our eyes have been shut
for a long time?

VANITY

Without hands
a woman would stand at her mirror
looking back only,
not touching, for how could she?
Eyelid.
Cheek.
Earlobe.
Neck-hollow.
The pulse points that wait to be dusted
with jasmine
or lavender.
The lips she rubs
rose with a forefinger.
She tends the image
she sees in her glass,
the cold replication
of woman,
the one
who dared eat
from her own hand
the fruit of self-knowledge.

EVE

kept to herself on the seventh day,
had everywhere
waiting to walk through,
so many new
names to see.
She could have spent all
of paradise looking,
just looking.

She leaned close to sproutings
and openings, cupping her palms
like a mouth around each
bud and setting-on fruit,

raising every first thing to her tongue,
licking the sound of it,
trailing her fingers in sand
while she memorized
how each word throbbed
as she uttered it,
standing a little ways off
to the side of the story.
Not wanting to be overheard.

(Shhh.
She's touching her lips
even now as she's
practicing, her fingers
smelling of spittle
and rose petals.)

COLD SPELL

I remember the stove's black belly
we huddled beside that afternoon,
the three of us,
two old and one young,
the wind whistling round the house.
It's the corners make it sing, my grandmother said,
the sharp edges.
The windows rattled,
the day outside bright as the sun on the Studebaker's
windshield I squinted toward
while they were dressing me
in my little white slip edged in lace,
and my little pink socks cuffed in lace,
and my Sunday-best dress with the hem
hitched up every two inches
so I could see more lace whenever
I sashayed around.
Because I was a girl.
I was their girl.
Their hands on my body were cold,
their mouths clicked and chirped.
The wind howled.

TRUNK

From its depths I could pull out
my grandmother's seersucker dresses and draw
them down over my little girl's body.

Photographs spilling from albums
I rearranged into new patterns,
not knowing whose stories I joined together

or cast asunder. Nobody ever came upstairs to scold
me for staying too long. From the styrofoam heart
that had stood at my grandfather's funeral

I unwound lengths of blue satin
and wrapped them like sashes around my waist.
Out of a Bible I shook loose some flowers

pressed thin as a butterfly's wings
and played bridesmaid preparing the way
for the woman enshrined in a painting

whose dirty glass I scrubbed with spit
on my shirtsleeves until I could see
who she was, my own grandmother gazing

down into a bouquet of lilies so lush
they unsettled me, trying to bloom their way
out of the staid composition.

MUSIC LESSONS

The last rose of summer, that sobbing old
song bubbling out of the piano keys,
not to mention the stalk of my grandmother's throat
as she played, made us stand like Victorian vases

waiting to be filled. (In the living room
dark as a museum, my ancestors gathered
in foliate frames, buttoned up to their chins.)
When I too became old, would I smell

like the rose water she liked to splash
on her neck and her wrists? Or like water in which
her cut flowers had stood for too long
on the dining room table? I lifted my wrist

to my nose. Soap and talcum powder.
Here comes the second verse, girls! So we opened
our mouths to the lure of that Irish air,
chirping of shadows that fell on a faraway garden.

As for her own garden rife with petunias
and blossoming okra plants, honeybees reveled
inside it all afternoon. But who listened? Not us,
still rehearsing the old endings loud as we could.

HER PORCH

Here she would pour out her hair
from her Sunday hat
and sit rocking the sermon away,

looking deep into shade beyond
fingerleaf ferns and mimosa leaves,
wanting none of us near for a little while.

Bread in the oven could wait,
the blackberry pies baked on Saturday night,
lying under a clean linen cloth.

We could all of us wait,
with our hungers she knew
only too well: through how many prayers

had she listened to each of them
grumbling, the stomachs
she'd feed when the service was over?

Whatever she saw in the shadows
those mornings when she shooed us out
to her garden to deadhead the roses

and sticky petunias, my cousins and I
became lost in it, making our way
through her jungle of tame floribunda

while she sat alone
in the peace of this empty house,
quietly forgetting our names.

CORRESPONDENCE

A teacher of grammar and penmanship,
she saved her letters
in chifforobe drawers or stacked
on the floor of her closet.
They lie even now where she left them.
Every last one of them answered.

I'd watch her bend over her desk,
words streaming onto the ivory vellum
like blue tributaries,
and sometimes, when she left awhile
to tend gumbo that boiled on the stove
or fold linens she scooped from the clothesline,
I touched those rose-scented sheets

and tried to imagine I lifted
their seamless meander of words
from the envelope.

When I complained over school compositions,
that I could find none of my own words
for such disagreeable assignments,
she would say, *Just pick a word*
and then wait.
Like a leaf spinning
round in a backwater,
sooner or later it catches the current.

Her last letters never got mailed.
When I read them,
her perfect blue words drift away
on a tide of forgetfulness,
as if she lived out her days underwater.

A few now and then break
the surface,
names of roses
she still pruned
and watered. King's Ransom.
Joseph's Coat.
Queen Elizabeth.

Not debris,
as a rescue team scanning the waste
might describe them,

but more like the named
things themselves,
as if she'd thrown them,
one by one,
into the wake
of her vanishing.

HANDIWORK

Everywhere I looked
I saw lace. Out the window
the lace of dead branches,
lace of an unraveling cloud,
every edge yearning
toward its disappearance

while inside
she sat hooking circles
of white thread
as if she remembered
how each stitch repeats
to make patterns
she no longer
knew how to finish.

No silver hooks now
for her. Or for me.
No old lady's mincing white
chain-stitches clinging like cobwebs
to every frayed surface.

I am done with this longing
for lace as a way of ending
things gracefully,
crochet and half-turn,

the teasing of filaments into
a border to prettify thresholds
too suddenly come upon.

This needs a touch of lace,
she'd say to nobody,
fingering the emptiness

while I squirmed at her side,
thinking, *Let the end
come, no matter how
ragged the finish.*

OPEN CASKET

For two days she lay
in our living room. That she never moved
chilled me more than the terror she might.

A stirring in the net curtains
over the shut window and I was wide
awake. What happened

after the last breath? The cotton-
stuffed silence of death,
did it last, or would angels begin

to trill louder than katydids,
the sinking sun burning a hole in the sky
through which I'd be borne heavenward?

ARIA

I lived for art, I lived for love. . . .
Why, O Lord, why
Dost thou repay me thus?

Listening to Callas sing
"Vissi d'arte" on a decades-old record,
I hear time scratching counterpoint
into the art of her voice.
La Divina, the liner notes call her,
as if she were deathless.

The Goddess herself,
it's true, crooned to us mortals,
but so long ago scarcely anyone
knows how she knelt to her work over
all that lies fallow beneath our feet.

Come evening, I'll hear
her chorus of frogs in the low
pasture, long after Tosca
has leapt to her death,
singing not for the glory of art
but for earthly awakenings

into another spring.
Thus does she sometimes repay
us, her stubborn joy rising
again out of thawed ground
like the breath from a diva's
throat spiraling into bel canto.

NOCTURNE

Chopin, my mother's favorite composer,
wrote dozens, inspired by moonlight
and the scent of a candlewick snuffed
by the wind through his wide-open window.

All she could play on the keyboard
was chopsticks.
No lessons for her.
They had gone
to the eldest girl,
who, of course, hated the instrument.

As did I,
forced to sit late afternoons
in the living room
practicing scales
or "The Carnival of Venice,"
breathing in furniture polish
and fuzz from the overstuffed sofa.

She wanted a daughter who could,
in her old age, play Chopin for her.
The Nocturnes.
Her favorites.

And if I contracted the polio
everyone feared, I could sit in my wheelchair
to play, and then wouldn't I always be grateful
I'd suffered through those school recitals
when I heard my fingers bolt off on a ride
of their own, over every wrong key?

After three years of lessons, I quit,
but I still feel my mother's hands
move as my own when I pick at my nails,
drum the table impatiently,
grasp this pen tightly as if she might,
even at this late an hour,
on this moonlit night,
make my fingers make music.

PEARLS

Lost in the summer dark,
the house waits as if
for my mother to come out
and sit on the porch, 1940 again,
with the war far away,
just like everything
else in the world beyond
her girlhood place
where the back roads
keep on going nowhere,
the lightning bugs kindling
the same feeble lights
as those she tried her best
to imagine were cities
that shimmered way off in the piney
woods, crickets beginning
to strike up a sort
of beguine, like an orchestra
playing at that very moment
in the Waldorf Astoria.
So let them begin.
Let my mother
sit down on the porch steps,
the radio's cord
reaching only as far
as the threshold,
and listen through static
to Glenn Miller swinging
his wand to the music of pearls
on an endless gold string.

{3}

—*O remember*
In your narrowing dark hours
That more things move
Than blood in the heart.
—Louise Bogan, from "Night"

DARK HOUR

Another day pours
itself into the bygone until
nothing's left

to be squandered.
Alone at my table
I'd not noticed mote

by mote
light disappearing.
Why not?

Night, at each
of my windows,
interrogates.

I raise my right hand
still clutching a half-eaten croissant,
my lap full of crumbs: I confess

I have drunk too much wine,
nibbled too many hors d'oeuvres. I confess
that, as always, I've reached for a second,

a third helping, wanting more
gravy, more meat
on my plate, not to mention

dessert, whether just
one more cookie or scoops
of whipped cream in a soup bowl.

I know I'm surrounded.
But I'm in no hurry to lay down
my fork and be bullied,

or spooked,
by Night's blank windows
shining my ghost faces back at me

when I look straight through
myself into darkness
before I extinguish the lights.

WEDDING

As always I sit in a back pew,
the easier to escape
once it's over.
Green spangles flounce
at the chapel's high glass.
Budding cherry trees sway
to the beat of the blooming
world's psalmody.

Wherever I look,
I'm the odd woman out.

If God had not grown
hard of hearing, I'd tell him
we old maids,
on average,
live longer than anyone else.
But He wouldn't believe me.

Man was not made to be solitary,
the preacher intones,
and this is why God ordained marriage.

Therefore we sweat
in the confines
of sacrament,
this bound to that,
man to woman,
blood to wine,
and so on
ad infinitum.

Outside the new leaves
can't stop surging
over the graveyard
where, side by side,
husbands and wives await
trumpets, the big send-off.

Meanwhile, his mouth full
of false teeth
and snuff,
his idle hands age-speckled,
God sits alone
in his canopy of stars.

EAVESDROPPING

He was trembling so
and his lips were turning blue,
she speaks into the pay phone
as I pass, in search of the ladies'
room hidden somewhere
in the hotel bar's posh
outer dark. I can't stop

myself wondering what was he
to her and why was he
trembling, his blue lips about to say
something this woman, struggling
to make herself heard over
happy hour, might or
might not be about to confide
as I shove my way through

the inevitable end
of her story and into
the door labeled *Mademoiselles,*
where a plush carpet,
rococo mirror
atop a pink vanity,
welcome me.

I pull out my lipstick
and slowly apply it to top lip,
then bottom lip.
Look at my mouth in the mirror.
The color I like,
extra long lasting.

No smears.
My hand's steady.
Nothing about my hand trembles.

WISTERIA

The hands. The secret lies in the hands,
the dancer from Andalucia explains
on the afternoon radio program,
and I wonder which
secret? The secret of everything opening
over and over again
every April? Even these windows,
sealed shut over too many winters,
through which I can smell the wisteria?

Soleares,
Seguiriyas—
the guitar strings throb
through the static and I feel
my spine arching,
arms begin twining
around me, my fingers seducing

the air. Stroking emptiness. Oh,
to be wrapped like a gypsy in endless black fringe
I would slowly unwind from my hips and let
fall to the floor. Kick it out of my way

and get on with the real work of dancing
this song to its end, drunk as always
I've wanted to be with the scent of these blossoming
vines that my mother said ought to be ripped
from a tree before they have enough time to kill it.

EL DÍA DE LOS MUERTOS

In Frida's house, it was every day.
She doted on skeletons,
contraptions of wicker and colored paper strung up
with twine, letting one hang alongside her bed
and another recline on her canopy. *Mis compañeros*,
she called them. *Compadres.*
She'd stared back at Death,
nose to nose,
frente a frente,
for so long she called him
El Viejo. Just part of
the household. She knew he would
nudge her too soon and say *Lista?*
Está lista, mi'jita?
No wonder she scrawled
on the last written page of her diary,
I hope the leave-taking is joyful
and I hope never to come back.

Forty years later,
I almost believe her.
It's November second again,
and again I imagine her grinding
her teeth on those last words
(despite being nothing but ashes
Diego sealed into a clay pot),
still trying too hard to resist the fiesta
that's dawning, its candy skulls hawked
from the corners, the jiggety-jig
of the bone-men in every mercado.

At nightfall, the cities of graves
with their pink vaults and blue stucco archways

will come back to life with the pictures of lost children,
wives, fathers, husbands, while flowers cascade
over gravestones where, nestled in baskets,
pan dulce and still warm tortillas
the living once loved to hold inside their mouths
keep the taste of life fresh for the dead
to come back to, if only as wind playing
over the grass, blowing
out every candle
before moving on again,
not having answered the question
we're left to ask, begging the darkness
that takes us, *Adonde? Adonde?*

NEMESIS

1.
Dark sister
I dread
like a trap

door, outsider
beyond
all good breeding

and common
sense, she knows
I listen: her satin

thighs slide
over horsehair as she
sidles closer.

Her scent?
The scorch after
lightning strikes.

2.
Who else would dare
twit the Old Man
when he thunders Let

There Be Light? Nothing
doing, she teases
him. She's been

around. She knows
what's coming. "Star-
dust," she whistles

as she files
her crimson nails,
making me wait

for the entrance
she wants, loving stealth
and the winding

way down
the dark stair
well on tip toe.

UNANSWERABLE

When I am gone from this house
will a coil of my silver hair navigate
stairwells and empty rooms
when there's enough wind to find it,
enough light to shine on my almost gone presence?
And if there should be such a shimmering,
who would be here to see it?
To notice my cups with their coffee stains
still in the bottom,
the clothesline that once held my wet garments
up to the sun,
to acknowledge my archive
of letters and
check stubs,
and lift to their noses
my soap dish
still caked with what welcomed
my flesh back to life
every morning?

BATHTUB

The body of an aging woman
is a memory.
—Eavan Boland, from "Anna Liffey"

I still paint my toenails.
The shade of the day?
Call it Passion Fruit.
Tomorrow, who knows?
Maybe Black Ice
or Ghost Orchid.

They tease like memory waiting
to float to the surface. The length of
my back laced with bath oil
and hair tumbled loose from
a chignon. My breasts rising out
of the shimmering suds. Every old woman
bathtub should offer such lush
retrospection: this body that used to be

all I can barely remember he wanted.
Oh you, he'd moan, twisting
my hair tight as I once myself gripped
the mane of my grandfather's
runaway horse while the sniveling
cousin who clung to my back
screamed for daddy. So I might

have used up my life wanting
only what somebody else
wanted. *Oh baby, I want*
you, he'd bury deep
in my ear. When he promised

me, *You'll want for nothing,*
I almost believed him.

Tonight I want nothing
but what any woman who's lived long
enough wants, to lay down
my body in rose-scented bathwater
lapping the rim of what holds me
and wiggle my succulent toes
as though passion could
still be made flesh
in an old woman's memory.

EARLY

Morning again,
again waking up, saying
the end of a poem
I read only last night,
There is nothing to keep us
from throwing ourselves
on the mercy of death
but desire. Again
wondering "What
now?" The windows
still open,
already the end
of September,
the last
day, the very last
day of my life
I will wake, saying
morning again.
Is there fog
or blue sky?
Have the birds gone
or come back?
I hear dogs howling
down by the river,
tires squealing,
somebody calling out *Come*
on, come on,
as if I have slept too long
through my life.

HOOT OWL

Don't call to me anymore.
I'm not listening.

Might as well
tell all the shadows it's time

to sneak out
of the woods, easy pickings

in here while I sleep, empty hands
on my breast

and my breath
barely stirring the air

as my open
mouth dreams in

and dreams out
more dreams

than I'll ever
need, each of them hungry

for who knows
what when I waken.

LISTEN

This old hymn
of April again,
dawn beginning the same
way my jewelry box
opens, its little tune tinkling
as the ballerina turns:

Here's my mother
come back to her vanity,
mulling which silver
chain hooked
round her neck
or her wrist,
which distillation
of light from her earlobes.
The day burns like fire
at her fingertips,

rousing the birds
to a reveille
I might as well conduct,
sprawled in my sheets,
wide awake as I am,
wanting words to this music

I know have been waiting
for me all my life
as if Jesus himself
might spit onto his fingers
and, touching my tongue,

whisper
Ephphatha,
Ephphatha! *

* *Open, open!* (Mark 7.34)

NIGHTCAP

Freeze warning.
Leaves curled on emptiness
crawl across

sidewalks. My gatepost
surrounded by wind jangles
nonsense.

I'll stay put
and kindle
some fat wood

with yesterday's
newspapers ripped to
confetti.

But what if the matches
won't strike, the chimney
won't draw?

What if this goose flesh
I hug to my breast
shivers not from the ice

waiting outside but inside
where no slug of whiskey
can thaw it?

Hush!
I'll take a jelly glass
down from the pantry.

Now stand back
while I pour a jigger
of bottomless fire

water,
straight-up.
Last call.

TIRED

Even as she honed her butcher knife,
she muttered, *Some days*
I want to stop dead
in my tracks and stand sniffing the air
like an old dog.

That was the last autumn she came
to hog-killing, so tired,
my mother said, you could smell
death trailing after her.

How does the odor of death
ride on wind?
Like a strip of confetti?
A crow's feather?
An old woman's nightgown
blown clean off the clothesline?

Who wouldn't rather smell
ferns quietly unclenching finger
by green finger
under the loblollies,
or lily-pads sculling
like open palms
over the fishpond?

I used to tend everything
she'd planted, even the roses
she left on the edges
of every last piece of our
property. But now,
when she wants to stop
dead in her tracks,

out of breath
on her stiffening legs,

I don't stop her.
I stand
till I feel how
she felt, standing there
smelling death
make its way
down the hog's belly
into black, soggy ground.

It's been years since I've kept a garden,
the soil needing too much work. One breath
of spring, and my old dread of late freeze
comes back again. Sometimes it's moonlight
that keeps me awake. Sometimes night sweats.
Then I feel a clamor like wings

in my throat. The most frightening sound? Wings
in the chimney or trapped in the house. Such a garden
of fears I've grown all my life, sweaty
stalks rising out of the muck! When I couldn't breathe
my mother would turn on the light
and sit rubbing my back. She spooned frozen

milk into my mouth, as if she'd freeze
the dark in my throat where those wings
trembled. The trouble with light?
There's never enough at the end. I imagine a garden
the dying walk into as they take their last breath
before the gates slam shut. These sweaty

deathbed imaginings! What good does it do me to sweat
if I've nothing to show for it? If I could freeze
time, I'd never forget how each next breath's
a mystery. What keeps it going, this wing-
beat of rise and fall, first thing that out of the garden
gate Adam and Eve saw, the cold light

of their own mortality dawning? God's light
seemed thrilling at first. They were glad to sweat
under it, tilling the soil of that first garden,
expecting good weather to last, not a hard freeze

in store for eternity. The angels dozed, wings
furled all afternoon. So silent. Scarcely a breath.

Some days the wind makes me catch my breath.
Then I'm amazed by the simplest things—light,
for example, or air, the way it's made for wings.
I remember my father at night washing sweaty
hands, dirt spinning round in the drain. He could freeze
me with one look, God turning me out of the garden.

That garden has always been breathing its myth
down my throat, its freezing light making my palms
sweat, my arms heavy with wanting to be wings.

EVE SINGS TO THE OKRA

Your last day and look
at you, boasting
your new flower, flimsy

as peau de soie,
dressed to the beaucoup
for Jubilee. *Bon soir*

before I uproot
you and dump you like cordwood
on top of the compost.

So sorry, *ma cherie,*
but nobody promised you September
lasted forever. Now don't pout

and don't play
for time, standing there
in the briefest of yellow

light, waving your green
fans and teasing me: Ooo la-la,
just one more night?

C'est la vie!
Let the wind take you.
Can't you feel frost

in the air?
Icy petticoats,
you can be sure

of it. Quick,
kiss the ants in your loving
cup bye-bye.

They'll have to leave,
taking the taste
of you elsewhere.

OPEN

Why do I turn to look back?
Let the dark keep itself to itself.
Let this house keep.
It's not going anywhere.

I am.
My handbag slung over my shoulder.
My left wrist aglitter with silver.
This hat that a young girl might wear,
why shouldn't I wear it?
Why shouldn't I swing the door wide and walk out?

The door on the other side's open,
the day blazing through
and beyond it another way
into which I might keep going
or disappear.

Vamanos!
Avanti!
Lightly,
lightly, I sing to myself,
shutting the door
ever after behind me.

Notes

Epigraph, Part 1
Marie Beaudry Lucas was born and educated in North Dakota but lived in North Carolina in her later years. The epigraph is taken from her collection *After Sixty-Five* (privately published, 1990).

"Early"
The italicized lines beginning "There is nothing . . ." are from Cecilia Woloch's "History," found in *Sacrifice* (1997).

"Open"
The lines "*Lightly, / lightly* " are taken from Randall Jarrell's "An English Garden in Austria":

> Then there is silence; a soft floating sigh
> *Heut' odor morgen kommt der Tag.*
> And how shall we bear it?
> > > > > > Lightly, lightly.

The German is a line from Strauss's opera *Der Rosenkavalier*. The Marschallin is speaking.